Original title:
What Remains of Us

Copyright © 2024 Creative Arts Management OÜ
All rights reserved.

Author: Grace Jackson
ISBN HARDBACK: 978-9908-0-0720-5
ISBN PAPERBACK: 978-9908-0-0721-2

The Weight of Silence

In a room so still, I hear a sneeze,
Dust bunnies dance like they own the keys.
The clock ticks loud, a mocking bird,
Each tick is a joke, oh haven't you heard?

The fridge hums soft with secrets untold,
A decade-old pizza, however bold.
Whispers of laughter hang in the air,
A ghost of a party, we were never there.

Lingering Footprints

Tiny prints in dust, they trace and weave,
A cat's nightly antics, you'd never believe.
Chasing shadows, thinking it's fun,
Yet I know for sure, it's my shoe that's done.

Outside in the yard, the kids ran wild,
Leaving behind treasures, oh so unstyled.
Half-eaten snacks like a breadcrumb trail,
Reminds me of stories of the great snail sail.

Remnants of Joy

A pickle jar full of mismatched pens,
Each has a story, oh where should I begin?
Crayons long lost in the depths of despair,
Waiting for someone to handle with care.

Laughter echoes in the corners so shy,
Memories stuck like a fly in the pie.
Leftover giggles swirl with the breeze,
Picking up footprints, if only they please.

Unfaded Letters

Old letters stacked like a game of jenga,
Words of a crush, oh the joyous benga.
Ink faded slowly but the giggles remain,
A memory parade of sweet awkward pain.

Scribbles of hearts in corners defined,
Each doodle a secret, cleverly entwined.
Years pass by but the paper won't shred,
Humor in heartaches, laughter we said.

Ballads of What Was

Once we danced like silly geese,
Spinning tales of our oddities,
Wit as sharp as a cardboard knife,
Laughing loud at each other's lives.

Time flies while wearing mismatched socks,
Our memories hiding in forgotten boxes,
Each giggle a snippet of what we knew,
Yet here we are, still chasing the view.

Silent Stones Beneath the Surface

The rocks pretend they know our jokes,
While turtles nod with knowing pokes,
Each ripple sings a lowly song,
Of all the quirks that keep us strong.

We giggle at the shadows cast,
By every choice we make too fast,
Yet in the silence, laughter blooms,
With stones as witnesses in the glooms.

The Aroma of Distant Affection

Ah, the scent of burnt toast wafts near,
Bringing memories sharp and clear,
Like that time you tried to bake a pie,
And we both ended up asking why.

Lost in the aroma of silly dreams,
We chuckle at life's weirdest themes,
Each flavor a reminder we can't ignore,
Of love that's messy, but never a bore.

Dust and Dreams Beneath the Stars

Beneath the sky where squashed dreams lay,
We laugh at the wishes that went astray,
Each star a laugh, each cloud a sigh,
As we rewrite our tales on the fly.

With every grain of dust that falls,
We trade our wisdom for silly calls,
In the cosmic dust of what has been,
Life's better with a laugh in between.

Fragments of Time

In the corner, dust bunnies dance,
Wobbling around like they've found romance.
Old socks laugh from their hidden den,
We wonder how they got there again.

A clock ticks on, but its hands disagree,
Time's a prankster, as wobbly as can be.
Our laughter echoes through this quirky space,
While memories trip and fall on their face.

The Essence of Us

We stumble through life, like two left feet,
In the kitchen, last night's leftovers we greet.
Our hearts are wild, covered in peanut butter,
Each hug's like a dance—awkward but no clutter.

We argue like pros over the last slice,
With verbal spatters that are precise.
Through joyful chaos, we boldly soar,
In the circus of life—our own encore.

Memories in the Air

In every whiff of burnt toast, I see,
A dance party from the time we were free.
Balloons from last year float high in delight,
They giggle at us, oh, what a sight!

The echoes of laughter still bounce off the wall,
Reading old notes with someone's bad scrawl.
Each scribble and doodle is a treasure we keep,
In the attic of moments, where friendships leap.

Whispers of the Past

Dusty old photos with silly grimaces,
Captured snapshots of our youthful phases.
We've mastered the art of making a mess,
Like toddlers in shoes that are far too small, yes!

Grand tales of failures that never grow old,
Are shared over popcorn, our secrets retold.
In friendly debate, our memories clash,
Never forgetting the time we both crashed.

The Stillness After

In the quiet of the night, we giggle,
As socks and shoes start to wiggle.
We spill some beans and drinks anew,
And wonder how the cat just flew.

The couch still holds our laughter loud,
While crumbs of snacks form a proud crowd.
The echoes of our silly chats,
Blend in with dreams of silly cats.

A Journey Left Behind

With luggage filled with socks and snacks,
We travel roads while dodging cracks.
Yet somewhere in that crowded bus,
A lost shoe whispered, "Eh, just us!"

The maps are all the same old lines,
Yet every stop gives us new signs.
As we step into the unknown rain,
We laugh at how we lost the train.

Imprints on the Soul

Our footprints dance on sandy shores,
While jellyfish shout, 'Please no more!'
We leave our prints, a silly trace,
Like toddlers after a cake-eating race.

The echoes of our folly stay,
While seagulls giggle and fly away.
In memories, we lightly tread,
With tales of bites from the cake we've fed.

Carried by the Winds of Change

The breeze blew in with quirky tunes,
As we chased after runaway spoons.
With hats askew, we spun around,
   Chasing giggles on the ground.

Leaves flutter down in silly spins,
While whispers share our secret sins.
As time rolls on, we laugh and play,
In funny hats, we'll find our way.

Ghostly Embraces

In the attic, dust bunnies dance,
They whisper secrets of missed romance.
Old chairs creak like gossiping friends,
Their stories echo, never quite ends.

Framed pictures grin with humor so dry,
Caught mid-gesture, as if to imply.
A sock on the floor with a tale of its own,
A ghost of a laundry day, forever alone.

Reflections in Still Waters

Puddles mirror the world, oh so clear,
Splash in them, laughter and joy reappear.
Frogs leaping high, with a splashy salute,
While ducks strut around in fanciful suit.

The moon's a joker in the night's big show,
Casting splashes of light in a rippling flow.
We laugh with the frogs, at our own silly plight,
Waltzing with shadows till the morning light.

Constellations of Memory

Stars winking secrets we used to share,
They giggle in clusters, a cosmic affair.
Comets streak by with a fleeting delight,
Leave trails of laughter in the depth of night.

A picnic blanket sprawled in the yard,
Ghost sandwiches wrapped, never too hard.
The silver spoon flies, oh, what a scene!
In the sky of our hearts, we laugh in between.

The Canvas of Lost Words

Crayons scribble on memories' face,
In a gallery of giggles, we find our place.
Each doodle a whisper, a chuckle, a cheer,
The paintings of us just dripping with queer.

A joke on the fridge from a magnet so bold,
Yellowing papers, our laughter retold.
Brush strokes of silliness flood the whole page,
As we grin like children, defying our age.

The Landscape of Silent Remembrance

In the fields where laughter fades,
Old socks dance like jolly parades.
We trace our steps through crumbs and jest,
As echoes linger, we find our rest.

Forgotten moments in a jar,
Riding bicycles, dreaming far.
With every chuckle, the past is drawn,
Like a cartoon, we'll carry on.

Cereal boxes tell our tales,
Of pirate ships and wind-filled sails.
In every hiccup of joy, we find,
The quirky shadows left behind.

Amidst the chaos, we stand tall,
Playing hopscotch through the hall.
In silent giggles, we reminisce,
Chasing memories wrapped in bliss.

Notes on a Broken Scale

Tick-tock goes the clock, oh dear,
The cat plays piano, but can't hear.
Notes fall flat like pancakes wide,
In this symphony, we can't abide.

Chasing ghosts of off-key song,
With a duck that quacks all day long.
Tunes that twist like pretzel dough,
Keep us laughing, oh what a show!

Each beat a blunder, each chord a tease,
Music notes dance like paper bees.
In quirky rhythms, we find the fun,
While shoes throw shadows, jumping, we run.

So, gather round the scale that's broke,
With wiggles, giggles, and some wild smoke.
In every flub, a chance to cheer,
Echoing laughter rings crystal clear.

Woven into the Silence

Threads of giggles line the air,
A tapestry of silly flair.
We stitch our lives with every pun,
In this quiet, we're all just one.

Oh, the socks that always mate,
In the dryer, they seal their fate.
Jumping jacks and silly hats,
The tales carry on, oh, just like cats.

Weaved in moments, fuzzy and bright,
Dancing looms 'neath a starry night.
With each stitch, a story spun,
Of mishaps grand and laughter fun.

So here's to silence, woven sweet,
In every tick, our hearts still beat.
Find the humor in the still,
As threads of joy, our souls fulfill.

The Abandoned Melodies

In a dusty corner, music lies,
Forgotten tunes and laughter cries.
A tuba squeaks, a trumpet sighs,
In this band, we wear our guise.

Old cassette tapes with tangled wire,
Play our anthems, set the fire.
With every scratch, a laugh erupts,
We dance like penguins, so corrupt!

The symphony of silly dreams,
Echoes of cake and whipped cream streams.
In every note, a fond embrace,
As melody wraps 'round the space.

So let's raise a glass to what's amiss,
In every blunder, a chance for bliss.
For in chambers of joy, we still reign,
Abandoned melodies, never in vain.

Footnotes in Time

In the jumble of our past,
Laughter echoes, shadows cast.
Forgotten socks and mismatched shoes,
We're the walking, talking news.

Every mishap, a tale to tell,
Burnt pancakes, oh, they worked so well!
Yet the joy in all those flops,
Are the gems that never stop.

Hats on heads and wigs askew,
Dancing like we haven't a clue.
With a giggle and a cheer,
We hold each other near.

So let's scribble footnotes bright,
In the margins of our light.
Through the silly and the wise,
Our humor never truly dies.

Songs of Silent Bonds

In the quiet, where we dwell,
Laughter resonates, all is well.
Whispers turn to songs of cheer,
Our silent bonds are loud and clear.

With a wink, we steal the show,
Invisible threads that ebb and flow.
In moments that seem plain and bland,
We find symphonies, hand in hand.

Old jokes shared beneath the stars,
Even mischief leaves no scars.
With every glance, a silent cue,
In this duet of me and you.

Life's a rhythm, funny and grand,
Every step, a tiny stand.
Through all the quirks and silly frowns,
Together, we wear laughter's crowns.

In the Quietude of Memory

In the stillness, stories brew,
Each chuckle holds a hint of glue.
Forgotten times with pastries burned,
In laughter's warmth, the heart has turned.

We trip on words and trip on feet,
Each mishap makes our bond complete.
With every slip and silly face,
We carve our way, a joyful trace.

In a crowded room, just us two,
We whisper jokes as shadows grew.
With every giggle, memories bloom,
Chasing away the grimmest gloom.

So let's bottle up this cheer,
With each echo that we hear.
In the quietude, we find our way,
Through laughter, forever we'll stay.

The Spirit of Together

In a jam, we dance and twirl,
Every mishap a flapping swirl.
With popcorn fights and movie nights,
Together, we scale laughter heights.

No matter the trials in our quest,
With silly hats, we're truly blessed.
In whispers shared and secrets spun,
In this circus, we're the fun.

Moments passed, a silly glance,
Turned to a wild, wacky dance.
With every nudge and little tease,
We craft a bond that's sure to please.

So here's to us in laughter's light,
Turning the mundane into delight.
Through all the chaos, near or far,
Together we shine, our own bright star.

Tattered Pages of Our Story

Our tale's written on napkins,
Spilled drinks and crumpled dreams.
We laughed till our faces hurt,
In the margins, quinoa schemes.

The cat tried to steal the script,
We needed a better plot twist.
Each chapter a friendly mess,
Where logic and laughter coexist.

In the Wake of Forgotten Laughter

Echoes dance on the ceiling,
As we reminisce in our chairs.
Looking for ghosts of giggles,
Tripping on our silly flares.

The sock puppet stole the scene,
In the cupboard, jokes still cling.
Chasing shadows of chuckles,
While the kettle starts to sing.

The Essence that Lingers

Whispers of snacks shared at midnight,
Crumbs left like breadcrumbs of bliss.
Floating on memories sweet,
In uneasy laughter's abyss.

An old joke resurfaces sly,
Like dust on our favorite toys.
Our scent wafts through old stories,
Perfumed with glitter and noises.

Notes from the Quiet After

Banter fades into silence,
Jokes tucked 'neath a blanket of dust.
Yet the punchlines are grinning wide,
With echoes that we still trust.

Life scribbled in doodle notepads,
Adventure beaten by mundane.
Yet in the quirks we find treasures,
As laughter seeps through the pane.

A Symphony of Echoes

In every empty can you see,
A melody of lost decree.
The laughter dances, sounds so bright,
While shifting shadows steal the night.

Footprints cover the old, wet sand,
Like misplaced toys from a child's hand.
Each giggle lingers, takes its flight,
Leaving behind the stars of night.

Whispers float on breezy trails,
Tickling us with ancient tales.
A burp from lunch echoes with glee,
As nostalgia grins like a bumblebee.

So here we stand, and all is near,
With ticklish dreams and hearty cheer.
For memories sing just like the sun,
With silly hats, we're all just one.

Keys to Forgotten Doors

There are keys we've lost but still have fun,
 Hiding in the pockets of the sun.
A door creaks open with a goofy grin,
 Revealing laughter from deep within.

Old chests contain socks, but not much gold,
 Each treasure, a story waiting to be told.
  Open with care, it might just bite,
  A rubber chicken waits for the light.

   Grandma's recipe sits all alone,
   Flour dances like a timid drone.
   A goblet of milk, a plate of pie,
   The tastes of old make the heart sigh.

We'll jiggle the knobs and turn the screws,
With quirks like these, who needs the blues?
  For in each creak, a memory sways,
  Our silly lives in a thousand ways.

Tides of Yesterday

The waves rolled in with a honking sound,
As seagulls dressed in funky gowns.
Yesterday's jokes spill from the shore,
Each splash a giggle we can't ignore.

Flipping through pages of sandy books,
A crab gives us all the funny looks.
Each tide brings back odd tales and puns,
Oh, how they tickle the setting suns!

Shells whisper secrets of silly fights,
With ghostly seafarers in strange tights.
The ocean grins with a cheeky jest,
While sending forth its salty quest.

So raise a toast to the funny waves,
For laughter hides in all the caves.
We ride the surf with smiles wide,
On silly tides, we take our pride.

Faint Traces of Touch

Fingerprints smeared on glassy walls,
Echoes of moments that giggle and call.
We play hide and seek with a wobbly chair,
Finding the giggles hidden somewhere.

Rug burns from tumbles and gleeful rolls,
Laughter erupts, filling up souls.
Tickles and cuddles, a clumsy dance,
Every stumble, a spark of chance.

Old toys scattered like bites of joy,
Each laugh a treasure from every girl or boy.
Under the bed, the whispers sigh,
Guarding the giggles that never die.

So let us cherish the faintest of touch,
In messy moments, they matter so much.
For in each embrace, a story ignites,
With funny remnants of our delightful nights.

Vestiges of Our Journey

In pockets of laughter we stash our quirks,
Tangled up memories, like old shirts with jerks.
We dance on the remnants of witty old pranks,
While pigeons are judging us, giving us ranks.

With socks that don't match, off we take flight,
Chasing our shadows in the shimmering light.
Like biscuits that crumble, we break and we blend,
In the showbiz of life, we're each other's own trend.

A fish in a bowl with a jigsaw-shaped grin,
We chuckle at moments, our mischief is kin.
Like echoes of chuckles that tickle the air,
In corners of chaos, we find treasures rare.

The runway of dreams is cluttered with wink,
As wiggly worms dance and the octopus sings.
In each giggle fit, we keep our own score,
The journey's the map, and we ask for encore.

The Beat of Ghostly Drums

Underneath the moon wearing socks that don't match,
We waltz with the spirits, the night's going to catch.
With ghostly fur coats and a poltergeist grin,
We tap to the rhythms of laughter within.

Our secrets like shadows parade through the night,
We tickle their fancy, give them a fright.
Like old mixtapes playing the songs that we shared,
In the orchestra of chuckles, no one is scared.

A hiccup of humor breaks silence in rows,
Goblins are giggling; our laughter just grows.
With beetles as dancers and owls on a drum,
We create a fiesta, a haunted old numb.

The fog offers hugs to the ruckus we bear,
With wisdom and whimsy, we twirl through the air.
For every lost giggle, a memory blooms,
Within the haunt of the past, our spirit resumes.

Breaths Between Us

With each inhalation, a chuckle's released,
Tinged with the scent of last week's burnt feast.
The pauses between us are filled with a grin,
As laughter entwines, and the chaos begins.

Like hiccups of joy, we bounce off the wall,
Trying to catch all of those moments that call.
A pancake that flops, or a shoe in a tree,
Each breath is a chance for pure ecstasy!

Our whispers are jams, like conspiracies sweet,
A recipe eats us, as we giggle and meet.
In breaths of connection, the silence decays,
And antics unfold through the whimsical maze.

With bubbles of laughter, we soar and we dip,
In the carnival of quirks, we never lose grip.
In fleeting exchanges, so funny and bright,
We float through the night on a cloud made of light.

Collapsed Worlds

In the junkyard of dreams, we find rusty toys,
A half-broken robot, it's lost all its joys.
With springs that are squeaky, we bounce through the mire,
Creating our chaos, igniting the fire.

Tangled up time in a misfit parade,
Where unicorns grin in the games that we played.
Like puzzles unfit, we make do with the mess,
Our laughter's the glue, and we've no need to stress.

As planets collide and the cosmos explodes,
We juggle the stardust, like motes on the roads.
The sandwiches float, and the pickles do dance,
In the dill of the void, we find our romance.

Within every fall, there's a giggle concealed,\nIn the slapstick of life, we can't be repealed.
With each trip we take, or a tumble we score,
We're stitched in the fabric, forever hardcore.

Fragments of a Shared Song

We danced under starlit skies,
Laughing till our sides would ache.
Each step a tune, a twist of fate,
In a chorus we forgot to make.

The echoes linger, sweet and loud,
Our voices joined in silly cheer.
A melody lost in the crowd,
Yet in dreams, I still can hear.

Notes are scattered like confetti,
In the air, they twirl and sway.
Moments passed, yet still so petty,
In our hearts, they find a way.

Fragments of laughter, pieced together,
Jokes we cracked on lazy nights.
Springtime blooms, bright as ever,
Chasing shadows, catching lights.

Outlines of Connection

Do you remember that wild trip?
With snacks piled high and seats askew?
Our roadmap turned into a slip,
But we found the fun in what we blew.

We charted paths, drew squiggly lines,
With scribbles no one could decode.
Every detour held funny signs,
Leading us down a wiggly road.

Your coffee spill, my juggling act,
We laughed until we nearly cried.
A tapestry of silly tact,
With threads of joy that won't subside.

Like puzzles missing half the pieces,
We mend the gaps with hearty jest.
In our game of life, love increases,
Because laughter always knows the best.

Silhouettes of What Was

In faded frames, we used to smile,
Shadows flickered on the wall.
A goofy pose, a wink, a style,
Insepems that continue to sprawl.

We wore the years like crazy hats,
Each chapter stacked with silly bliss.
Like silly cats, we chased the rats,
In moments we often miss.

Hiccups in the stories told,
Turned laughter into treasured gold.
A slip, a trip, the antics unfold,
In every tale, traces bold.

The jesters that we used to be,
Left whispers dancing in the light.
In silhouettes, we're wild and free,
In memory's lens, we shine so bright.

Untold Stories of Us

Amidst the quirks, our tales reside,
In every chuckle, in each sigh.
The road trips filled with joy, the ride,
With snacks and secrets shared on high.

That time you tripped, the ice was slick,
We laughed until our cheeks turned red.
You told me jokes, a clever trick,
A tapestry of gags we spread.

Unwritten stories wrapped in jest,
From all the times we tried to fly.
Each blunder left us quite impressed,
With memories that never die.

So here's to us in every laugh,
Our sketches won't fade away.
In every moment, we carve our path,
The funny bits are here to stay.

Imprints of Love's Footsteps

You left your socks in my drawer,
A scent I can't ignore.
Each step we took, a little grin,
Faded notes where love begins.

Coffee stains on my old shirt,
Your laughter bubbles, flirts.
A dance in the kitchen, quite a sight,
We waltzed with flour, oh what a night!

Forgotten snacks beneath the bed,
Gummy bears, where dreams are fed.
A trail of crumbs, oh sweet delight,
Chasing love through every bite.

Yet here we are, a joyful mess,
Collecting quirks, a true success.
As time rolls on, we both can see,
The joy in our sweet parody.

The Untold Tapestry of Us

Threaded laughs in every seam,
Stitches of a wild daydream.
A patchwork quilt of all we share,
Lopsided hearts and mismatched flair.

You find my keys in strange places,
Your smile lights up my grumpy faces.
With every tease and playful jab,
Life's a circus; we're the fab!

In tangled yarn, we twirl and tangle,
Every knot, a sweet mangle.
With every thread of fabric spun,
We weave a tale of endless fun.

Forgotten sketches on the wall,
Doodles of a dance hall brawl.
In scribbled lines, our story flows,
Through ups and downs, it brightly glows.

Vestiges of a Faded Embrace

Your old hoodie on my chair,
Faded memories fill the air.
A wrinkle here, a tear in seams,
In every stitch, a thousand dreams.

We argue over pizza crust,
Your secret stash, a must!
Wiggly worms in pants that fit,
Every crease a little wit.

Notes left stuck on the fridge door,
Love reminders, who could ask for more?
Odd socks dancing in lazy claps,
A portrait drawn of our mishaps.

Yet as time tricks us to play,
Life's little quirks make brighter days.
With laughter bounding, hearts embrace,
In funny moments, we find our place.

Time's Residue on Intimate Corners

Dust bunnies in the hallway roam,
Collecting tales from our shared home.
Each corner holds a whispered plight,
A cozy nook with silly bites.

Crumbs of kisses fall like rain,
Every sprinkle, part of our gain.
Lost TV remotes on silly quests,
In soft chaos, we find our jest.

Pajama days with hair in knots,
Every laugh, we glassy plot.
In mixed-up socks and silly hats,
We cradle love where laughter chats.

With time's soft touch, it's clear to see,
In every mess, you fit with me.
A joyful cheer through thick and thin,
In life's great show, we wear a grin.

Flickers of Forgotten Laughter

A sock lost in the washing spree,
Whispers tales of our mystery.
Leftovers in the fridge might sprout,
But hey, guess what the smell's about!

Old photos stuck in dusty frames,
We pose, we laugh, yet play strange games.
Like that one time we danced in the rain,
The neighbours still pretend they're sane.

A joke that fizzled, a pun that's flat,
We chuckle 'til we almost splat.
Echoes linger where laughter bloomed,
In a world of chaos, we're still resumed.

So raise a glass to silly schemes,
To stunted jokes and stretchy dreams.
For in the mess of our little fuss,
Lies the joy of all that was us.

Remnants of Unspoken Words

Your tea's too strong, mine's just right,
Whispers linger through the night.
We giggle over silent texts,
While the cat seems to know what's next.

Forgotten puns and silly rhymes,
Stored like old socks in ancient times.
A chuckle caught in awkward stares,
In this silence, our heart declares.

Unsaid thoughts like bubbles burst,
In the air, our laughter's first.
Each moment counts, though never said,
Like the ghosts of words that fled.

We stumble through our mute ballet,
In every pause, we find a play.
So here's to the speech left undone,
In the quiet, we still have fun.

The Distance We Traverse

We measure miles in silly dances,
In the chaos, we find our chances.
Like a marathon of mismatched socks,
We run in circles, in laughs we're boxed.

Each hello a step, each goodbye a leap,
Through the cracks, our memories creep.
A hopscotch game played in the air,
Our legs get tangled, but we don't care.

The road is long, with potholes too,
We skip and sway, in colors so blue.
Chasing shadows, we race the sun,
In this mad dash, we've already won.

With every bump, our laughter shines,
Over hills our silly heart aligns.
For distance folds when hearts are near,
And every step turns grins to cheer.

Eclipsed by Time

Tick tock goes the clock so sly,
While we joke and let moments fly.
Time can't catch our silly prance,
In the shadows, we still dance.

Doodles fade, as do old trends,
But laughter's echo never bends.
We stumble through the years like pros,
With each misstep, our humor grows.

Old trends may frown, and fashion's bleak,
Yet in the mess, it's fun we seek.
For every wrinkle tells a tale,
In the fabric of life, we shall not pale.

In every tick, our spirits thrive,
Through the grind, we still arrive.
With smiles bright to chase away grime,
We laugh together, eclipsed by time.

The Art of Letting Go

A sock left behind in the dryer,
Once a pair, now a lone flyer.
They dance their own little jig,
While we wonder about the big gig.

The keys that hide beneath the couch,
Laugh at our frantic search, they slouch.
Who knew they'd develop a flair,
For making us think they just don't care?

Old takeout hiding in the fridge,
Starts a new life, a furry bridge.
Like memories we can't quite toss,
Now it's a moldy, cheesy boss.

We wave goodbye, shed a tear,
For all those things we hold dear.
But let's face it, it's not so bad,
Life's a circus, and we're the glad.

Silent Testimonies

A coffee stain on the rug's right flank,
Whispers a truth that we never rank.
Each spill a moment, a tale untold,
Of nights too wild or too bold.

The fridge hums tunes of forgotten feasts,
While leftovers become the dark beasts.
What started as a gourmet delight,
Now haunts our dreams till morning light.

Dust bunnies roll, a furry brigade,
Puppets of indecision, we're afraid.
Who knew that cleaning could be such a game,
With dust collecting, it's never the same.

The silence speaks louder than a shout,
Echoes of laughter, shadows of doubt.
We navigate chaos, a dance in the dark,
Finding the humor in every quirk.

Threads of Connection

The tangled cords behind the desk,
Whisper "I love you" but feel grotesque.
Next to them, a forgotten remote,
Hiding secrets, sometimes a goat.

Old photographs of silly poses,
Capture smiles like blooming roses.
But as we glance, we see the hair,
Once so grand, now just a scare.

Messages left unread on the phone,
A testament to how we've grown.
We laugh at our past with a wink, a nod,
As we reminisce on what was odd.

With every connection, a thread we weave,
Ultimately leading to what we believe.
In the chaotic tapestry that we hold tight,
We find our joy in the absurdity of life.

The Space Between

A missing puzzle piece on the floor,
Giggles of joy and dread, what a score!
It hides in shadows, a bit of a tease,
Like a ghost in the attic that knows what we squeeze.

Between the laughs and awkward silences,
There's a dance of quirky alliances.
Whether it's a pun that lands or flops,
We cherish the moments till the fun stops.

Forgotten songs we sing off-key,
Resound in echoes like a wild spree.
They remind us that life's a silly ride,
Full of notes that we can't quite hide.

In all the gaps where silence slips,
We find our joy in the little quips.
For all that's lost, there's still enough cheer,
With humor and love, we persevere.

The Ghosts We Carry

In the attic, old shoes seem to hide,
A pair of mismatched socks, they confide,
Whispers of laughter from long-lost days,
We stumble on memories, in comical ways.

A ghostly chair that squeaks on its own,
With each creak and sigh, it hones a new tone,
A dance in the dusk, with shadows that tease,
We twirl with the echoes, just doing as we please.

The cat makes a fuss, with no one in sight,
Chasing the phantoms that give him a fright,
Yet we all know, through giggles and sighs,
These ghosts we carry are a fun surprise.

So let's toast to the days when we trip and we fall,
And those silly old spirits—they've got it all!
For laughter and memories never grow old,
In the attic of life, there's magic untold.

Roots Beneath the Surface

Deep down in the soil, a tangle of jest,
Roots intertwine, they're having a fest,
Planting stories in rows, like a witty parade,
With vegetables laughing, in sunlight arrayed.

Potatoes are thriving, with skins full of cheer,
Carrots playing hide-and-seek with a sneer,
Beneath all the dirt, their jokes intertwine,
Growing together, they're simply divine.

Above ground, we frolic while roots have their fun,
In the dance of the earth, they're second to none,
Who knew underground had a comedic flair?
The roots beneath us sing tunes in the air.

So dig in the garden, where laughter does bloom,
Among leafy greens, let's banish the gloom,
For while we may see just the tops of the scene,
The roots beneath wiggle, in laughter unseen.

The Trace of Love

Love leaves a mark, like a chocolatey hand,
Sticky and sweet, in a mess we had planned,
In the kitchen, we giggle, flour in the air,
A recipe of laughter, it's fun to prepare.

The socks in the dryer, they vanish in pairs,
Like love on a Saturday, no one really cares,
It's a game of mischief, it's playful and light,
As we chase socks, we laugh through the night.

We built paper forts, where dreams could reside,
With crayons and hearts, we let love be our guide,
Every doodle and scribble, a tale yet to weave,
In the mess of our making, we choose to believe.

So cherish the traces, both silly and bright,
In the scrapbook of life, let's bask in the light,
For love isn't perfect; it's messy and fun,
With each little trace, we become more as one.

Imprints on the Heart

Life leaves its prints, just like flip-flops do,
In the sand of our journey, we chuckle anew,
Footprints that wander, like ducks in a row,
A parade of our blunders, together they flow.

Memories squish like jelly on toast,
Sweet and so funny, it's laughter we boast,
We'll stick to the moments that poke at our sides,
These imprints of joy, where absurdity rides.

With splashes of paint from a clumsy old brush,
We color our stories in a colorful rush,
Every mark tells a tale, each giggle a part,
Of all the bizarre ways we're caught in the art.

So cherish those moments, as silly as they seem,
In the gallery of life, let's dance and just dream,
For imprints on hearts are a joyous surprise,
A wonderful mess that forever complies.

Journeys Written in Stardust

We packed our dreams in a suitcase,
Chased the moon in a hurry.
Fell over stars, made quite a mess,
Laughed so hard, our vision got blurry.

With cosmic dust in our hair,
We danced on Saturn's rings.
Told the sun we didn't care,
As we sang off-key, offbeat things.

Aliens joined for the ride,
Trading snacks in zero-gravity.
There's no place for pride,
When floating is your reality.

As comets waved us goodbye,
We promised to come back and play.
But space is vast, and so we fly,
To find more stardust along the way.

Whispers on the Edge of Memory

I recall a dance in the rain,
With hot dogs tossed like confetti.
We slipped and slid, what a strain,
Laughter echoed, oh so petty.

The ice cream melted on our nose,
As we giggled 'til we cried.
Life's little quirks, who really knows,
Why we slipped on fate's own slide?

You said, 'Remember when we tripped?'
I said, 'Remember that awful fall?'
In the park, our dreams had flipped,
But who tripped more? Me or you, after all?

As time ships sail through the fog,
We sketched our tales in the dew.
Memory's a fickle old dog,
Yet its joy always clings to you.

The Aftertaste of Us

After dinner, what a treat,
We shared a plate of mashed potatoes.
Dished on secrets, oh so sweet,
With each scoop of our old projigos.

Laughter mixed with spilled coffee,
As burnt toast became our art.
Every crumb told a story,
Of a friendship that warms the heart.

You swore the cake was divine,
But the frosting, oh what a flop.
Swapped tales over cheap wine,
Not a single regret, not a drop.

As the plates piled high and deep,
We laughed at our culinary crimes.
In the aftertaste, secrets keep,
And we both know the best punchlines.

Traces of Unraveled Threads

We wove our tapestry of quirks,
Knitting joy with tangled yarn.
Mistakes became our funny perks,
Each stitch a laugh, never a scorn.

Buttons lost and seams that fray,
A wardrobe of misfit attire.
Dressed in colors that shout 'Hey!'
Fashion faux pas that inspired.

Remember when we sewed our fate?
Made a couch out of pure wish thinking.
Sat on it, now isn't that great?
As it crumbled, we kept blinking.

In the chaos, we found the thread,
Of laughter threaded through our days.
With all the mischief, just like bread,
Life's best moments are the ones that play.

Afterglow of We

Sunshine smiles, they linger still,
Ice cream drips, a tasty thrill.
Laughter echoes in the hall,
We can't erase it, not at all.

Dusty socks in a tangled heap,
Silly secrets we dare to keep.
Tickled pink, we dance around,
In this chaos, joy is found.

Chasing shadows, giggles flare,
Sticky fingers, folly rare.
In the mess, our hearts align,
Finding treasures in the pine.

Kites that soared and fell from grace,
Mismatched shoes in a silly race.
From the playful, we're never free,
Each silly moment, soars with glee.

Leftover Moments

Crumbs of laughter on the floor,
Pizza boxes by the door.
Forgotten socks, a cheerful mess,
In chaos, we find our best.

Leftover jokes, they still will shine,
In the fridge of a blissful time.
What's that smell? Oh, it's our fun,
Half-eaten cupcakes from the run!

Faded photos on the wall,
Capturing moments, big and small.
Silly faces, we pose and grin,
With these relics, we always win.

Jumbled thoughts in our shared head,
Hungry laughter, we slice and spread.
Leftovers fill our hearts' delight,
In those crumbs, we spark our light.

The Tether of Time

Tick-tock goes the silly clock,
We dance around like a gagging flock.
In every tick, there's gagging cheer,
Moments freeze, sometimes unclear.

Slipping on time's silly face,
Trips and falls in a clumsy race.
With wobbly steps, we find our pace,
In the chaos, we embrace grace.

Balloons that float and then deflate,
Hiccups of laughter, we celebrate.
In the blink, a moment's gone,
Yet in our hearts, the joy lives on.

Time's a hug that's tight and snug,
Tangled tales, we pull and tug.
In every twist, there's charm galore,
In our giggles, we'll explore.

Souvenirs of Togetherness

Dusty trinkets fill the shelf,
Silly doodles of ourself.
Coffee cups with sassy quotes,
A memory that softly floats.

Fuzzy sweaters, mismatched pairs,
A treasure trove of laughs declares.
Tickets stubs from goofy shows,
In every heart, our friendship grows.

Lost in time amongst the bags,
We share giggles, sell our rags.
Holding hands on crowded streets,
In this jumble, life repeats.

Souvenirs of endless glee,
A treasure map for you and me.
Together, we write our legacy,
In these gifts, we'll always be.

Faded Pages

Our jokes are like old stains, not quite gone,
Each laugh a faded imprint, somehow drawn.
Scribbles in the margins of our crazy tales,
A quirky library where humor prevails.

We tripped through life, with socks mismatched,
Our plans like spoons, forever detached.
Yet in this chaos, a dance we find,
Like faces in clouds—a laugh intertwined.

Old photos hang like ghosts on the wall,
Each smile a riddle, we can't help but call.
With coffee spills and donut fights galore,
Our memories stick like gum on the floor.

In laughter's echo, our story's spun tight,
With silly adventures, we soar to new heights.
These faded pages hold treasures so bright,
In the library of life, we laugh through the night.

Treasures of the Heart

In pockets we carry our trinkets and dreams,
A rubber band ball and old silver beams.
Each knick-knack tells tales, oh so absurd,
Like the time we mistook a cat for a bird.

Our treasures are odd, but they sparkle with glee,
A shoelace, a key, a forgotten recipe.
Each object a chapter, rehearsed just for fun,
Like trying to dance when we completely can't run.

In the attic of memories, we giggle and hide,
A hat that once fit, now a comfortable ride.
With treasures so wacky, our hearts play along,
Like a karaoke night when you just can't sing strong.

From rubber ducks to old socks without mates,
Our hearts hold the bizarre, nobody debates.
In laughter we stumble, in joy we depart,
These quirky old treasures are true works of art!

Whispers in the Wind

A breeze carries whispers, oh, what do they say?
Maybe they gossip about yesterday's play.
With laughter that dances like leaves in the air,
Our secrets outsmart even the sun's golden glare.

In windy delights, our silliness sings,
Like kites in a chase, we embrace silly things.
Each gust wraps around us, tickling our cheeks,
As we trade goofy looks through the soft summer weeks.

The trees are our witnesses, vowing to keep,
The laughter, the mishaps, not too deep.
While echoes of giggles swirl behind us,
We skip down the path, totally fuss-less.

In soft whispers of wind, our joy floats away,
No matter the distance, we're here to stay.
These moments grow fonder, like clouds that won't rain,
In the breeze, we find joy that dances again!

The Fabric of Us

Stitched together with laughs and a thread of bright yarn,
Our quilt is a patchwork, full of quirks and charm.
Misfits and marvels, each square like a joke,
A tapestry woven till we giggle and poke.

With buttons for eyes and a tattered sleeve,
Each piece tells a story you wouldn't believe.
From paper mache dreams to glittery schemes,
Our fabric holds secrets and wild, silly themes.

We tango with socks that danced out of sight,
Twirling our mishaps, the snags feel just right.
Through stitches that tangle, we find the delight,
Each knot in our quilt makes our laughter ignite.

In the fabric of life, we create our design,
With stitches so silly, our hearts intertwine.
From holiday cheer to everyday fuss,
We're snug in this quilt—oh, the fabric of us!

Between Shadows and Light

In the dance of a shadow, we trip,
With laughter that echoes, a playful quip.
We stumble on secrets, hidden and bright,
In the chaos of day, we wiggle with delight.

The sun spills its warmth, but we lose our way,
Chasing the fun of our evening ballet.
With each slip and slide, a giggle ensues,
In a world made of light, we choose to amuse.

Who knew awkward could be such a thrill?
We chuckle at fate, with a wink and a spill.
In the spaces between, we embrace our own fun,
Celebrating the mishaps, oh, how we run!

Between whirls of laughter, our stories unfold,
In moments of mischief, our hearts turn to gold.
As shadows retreat and the moon starts to rise,
We dance with the light, under starry skies.

The Poetry of Absence

In the room where you laughed, now echoes remain,
Your joke on the tip of my tongue, like a train.
Though you're absent, your spirit still plays,
In the slight pauses, where chaos conveys.

I misplaced my keys, but got lost in your tales,
Swapping my sighs for our long-lost mails.
With every "Remember when?", laughter does flow,
Into voids and behind doors, where mischief may grow.

Missing out on your puns feels quite like a game,
I wear your absence like an award, not a shame.
In the silence that lingers, your antics appear,
With every good punchline, I'm left chuckling here.

So here's to the laughs that adorn empty chairs,
To moments that linger, our unspoken affairs.
In the poetry of absence, you thrive with a twist,
For in every sweet memory, I know you exist.

Hearts Adrift

Our hearts are like boats on a whimsical tide,
Drifting in circles, with nowhere to hide.
With laughter as oars, we paddle through life,
Navigating quirks, mischief, and strife.

In every bump, there's a giggle that chips,
As we sail through our day with unexpected flips.
We're lost on the maps that we scribble and draw,
Yet, in this confusion, there's always a ha-ha!

Our compass is skewed, yet we steer with flair,
Trading worries for chuckles, with jokes that we share.
With each sway of our vessels, we find sense of fun,
In this heart-shaped ocean, we merrily run.

Though the winds might be wild, in our hearts, we're bold,
We weather the storms with humor, and gold.
And as we drift on, like leaves on a stream,
We laugh as we float, in this absurd little dream.

Seeping into Yesterday

Memories seep like coffee stains, quite strange,
Spilling over laughter, in moments we change.
From shadows of giggles that wiggle and sway,
To remnants of joy that refuse to decay.

I find socks on the floor, a puzzling sight,
A reminder of chaos that feels just right.
In the mess of our days, much fun can be found,
In the clutter and splendor, we're spinfully bound.

As echoes of laughter sneak under the door,
They jiggle like jelly, and giggle some more.
In the fabric of time, we weave our own bliss,
With threads full of chuckles that no one can miss.

So let the clock tick while we frolic and spin,
In the soft glow of dusk, chuckling within.
As yesterday's whispers become our delight,
We'll dance with the past, hearts soaring in flight.

Echoes of the Unsaid

In the corners of laughter that never bloomed,
We shushed our secrets, the jokes we assumed.
Whispers of punchlines now float in the air,
Like socks in the dryer—do they even care?

The witty comebacks lost in the fray,
Their absence a dance in a silly ballet.
While we ponder our choices, we chuckle and sigh,
At the ghosts of our humor that just won't die.

Each raised eyebrow tells a tale of our past,
Where we stumbled and tumbled, oh how we laughed.
Now echoes of giggles linger like frost,
A reminder of days that we thought would get lost.

Yet here we stand, with our memories bright,
As we gather around for one more silly night.
The unspoken jokes like balloons in the sky,
Pop one and you'll find the rest flutter by.

The Last Breath of Our Dawn

Morning coffee spills, a ritual so grand,
We argue the weather as we both take a stand.
The sunshine may linger, but so does the jest,
Over toast that's too burnt, we humor our quest.

The last breath of dawn, a giggle ensues,
Our dreams weren't the same, yet we both share the blues.

We trip over pillows, a dance made of sighs,
In the chaos of life, we find our surprise.

Chasing the moments, now fleeting and fast,
Yesterday's humor is a blast from the past.
But as long as we're here, we'll tickle our fate,
With laughter that echoes, it's never too late.

So here's to the dawns, the messes, the fun,
Rewards that are endless, like warmth from the sun.
In every last breath, may we find a new way,
To laugh at our antics, come what may.

Remnants of a Shared Journey

Traveling together, our luggage was light,
Packed full of giggles and snacks for the flight.
The map was a riddle, a puzzling quest,
Finding routes of mischief, we did our best.

From airports to motels, our jokes took a spin,
We laughed as we chased the places we've been.
While the world turned to gray, we colored it bright,
With remnants of laughter that stole the limelight.

Lost keys and mishaps became part of the tale,
Every curb we stumbled on, we'd just set sail.
For fortune is laughter and mischief's our guide,
In uncharted waters, we still take the ride.

So here's to our journey, wherever we roam,
A comedy show for the hearts we call home.
In the remnants of travel, our spirits will shine,
With echoes of joy, oh how we entwine.

The Ghosts of Our Laughter

In the halls where we giggled, shadows take flight,
The ghosts of our laughter still dance through the night.
They tickle the corners of every old room,
Filling the silence with joy's playful zoom.

Silly faces and stories, like candies, we share,
Sweet bursts of delight filling up every air.
As time slips away, never missing a beat,
The ghosts of our chuckles make memories sweet.

In pictures adorned with odd hats and glee,
We haunt our own pasts, daring others to see.
For in every snicker, a spirit still gleams,
While laughter lingers, we'll chase all our dreams.

So here's to the echoes of giggles and fun,
The ghosts of our laughter, forever we run.
Through life's silly maze, may we never forget,
That joy's not a prize, but a constant duet.

In the Echo Chamber

In a room full of laughter, we raise a cheer,
Echoes of joy dance, and disappear.
Each joke like a bubble, they float and then pop,
Leaving us giggling, we just can't stop.

Mirror, mirror, on the wall,
Who's the most funny of them all?
The voices ricochet like a ping-pong ball,
Yet here we stand—did we really recall?

Gags from the past come creeping in,
Witty retorts lose to foolish grins.
Yet in this chamber, it's all just a game,
Where every lost word still knows your name.

So here's to the echoes, the laughs that we share,
In this snug little bubble, we float without care.
Stored in our hearts like a favorite song,
We'll cherish these moments—where we all belong.

The Color of Longing

Chasing rainbows on a Tuesday morn,
We paint our dreams, slightly worn.
With hues of hope and shades of doubt,
Our palette's a mess; there's no way out!

Each brush stroke whispers sweet, silly tales,
Of sunburnt days and windblown gales.
But hey, who needs color when gray's in style?
Let's dip in the jar and stay for a while.

Color me happy or color me blue,
Each tone's a reminder of things we can do.
But as the sky darkens, our laughter's ablaze,
In this world of longing, we'll dance through the haze.

Forget the picture, it's all just a game,
We'll mix all the colors; it's never the same.
In this swirling canvas, with each splash we scream,
Longing's just another palette in our dream.

Distant Horizons

The sun sets low on horizons unseen,
Where distant giggles paint everything green.
We dream of adventures in faraway lands,
With maps made of coffee and pizza in hands.

In the blur of the sunset, we chase silly dreams,
Sailing on laughter, or so it seems.
But the waves we ride are just puddles of thought,
Splashing around, we're all getting caught!

Far beyond mountains that tickle the sky,
With every horizon, we reach out to try.
But do we get farther, or just circle back?
As we laugh at ourselves, in our merry little track.

For each chuckle and grunt, a distant new view,
Turns mundane moments into something askew.
So here's to the journey, wherever it leads,
In the light of our laughter, our hearts plant their seeds.

The Palette of Memory

In the corner of my mind, colors swirl bright,
Shades of sweet laughter, all taking flight.
Pastels of stories in a watercolor haze,
Each vibrant memory, a laugh on display.

With a twist of a brush, I paint the absurd,
Life's little moments that often go unheard.
Like pie on the ceiling or a dog in a hat,
These colorful memories make me laugh, imagine that!

The canvas of living is splattered with cheer,
Every drip and every splash brings me near.
As I blend all these moments, it's clear to see,
What's left of my days is pure jubilee.

So dip in the pot, let your worries go dry,
In the palette of memory, we soar and we fly.
Each shade holds a giggle, a tinge of delight,
In the bright world of laughter, everything feels right.

Fragments of Echoed Whispers

In the attic, dust bunnies play,
With socks that wandered far away.
A teacup chatters to a spoon,
As if they'll dance beneath the moon.

Old comics giggle, pages torn,
They reminisce when we were sworn.
The cat breaks in, with a sly grin,
And claims the spot right where we've been.

A mirror laughs at hair gone wild,
Reflecting back the dreams of a child.
Forgotten shoes, the ones with flair,
Still hope to dance, but no one's there.

Echoes whisper in silliness,
Of what we lost in our own mess.
Yet in the clutter, joy's not far,
For laughter's light, it's who we are.

Shadows of Yesterday's Heart

The calendar's stuck, it's yesterday's news,
With chuckles slipping through the shoes.
We wore the past like a favorite hat,
A little too tight, but imagine that!

Leftovers dance in the fridge's glow,
Like we're hosting a party no one will show.
We toast with our cups, half-full and bold,
As shadows chuckle, both young and old.

A harmony of socks without their pairs,
In this playful ballet, no one cares.
Collages made from snippets and threads,
Life's oddities pile up by our beds.

But amidst the whispers, we find delight,
In the quirky tales spun each night.
For shadows of yesterday wear a grin,
Reminding us how the fun begins.

The Silhouette of Lost Dreams

Lost in the corners, they frolic and play,
Like kites that soared but drifted away.
A fridge magnet asks for a second chance,
While shadows peek in for a curious dance.

Old diaries giggle, with secrets untold,
Of crushes all silly, and adventures bold.
A pillow might smirk if it could recount,
The dreams whispered softly, that still amount.

Socks with holes tell tales of the past,
Of races and tumbles, joys that won't last.
A sock puppet laughs, with a goofy smile,
As the sunlight drapes over our little pile.

In the shadows, we find a jest,
Those lost dreams often give us rest.
For laughter sprouts in the most absurd,
Our silly silhouettes in a world that's blurred.

Memories Woven in Time

Threads of laughter weave through the years,
Like a jester juggling our joyous fears.
Each moment's stitched with a quirky thread,
In a tapestry bright where no one's misled.

The clock ticks backward, but that's just fine,
As we sip on stories brewed like wine.
A clock's silly face with its wide-open grin,
Looks forward to parties it once helped begin.

Odd trinkets clink with a hilarious tune,
Each remembers the night we danced with a broom.
And moments unwrapped like gifts just for laughs,
Bring silliness back, like our goofiest crafts.

In the fabric of time, the fun never ends,
As we stitch memories, beloved friends.
For these woven tales will forever stay,
In the laughter that bubbles throughout our play.

Ashes of Our Shared Nights

In the kitchen, crumbs still dance,
Leftovers sing of our last romance.
The cat snores deep on the couch,
While we laugh about that silly grouch.

Our socks are mismatched, a colorful spree,
A collection of chaos, just you and me.
Forgotten coffee cups line the floor,
Each sip a giggle, who could ask for more?

Your old records spin tales of the past,
We dance like fools, a rhythm so fast.
The walls still echo our silly fights,
In the shadowed corners, our love ignites.

These moments are etched in the fluff of the chair,
Where we plotted dreams, without a care.
Even now, as the daylight descends,
In laughter and warmth, our story transcends.

The Map of Uncharted Heartbeats

We scribbled our dreams on old napkin sheets,
With doodles of journeys and outlandish feats.
A treasure map leading to marshmallow land,
Where laughter and giggles go hand in hand.

A compass that points to the fridge in the night,
With snacks that glow in the moon's soft light.
Our hearts beat wildly to a quirky tune,
In the dance of the stars, we're marooned to the moon.

Each heartbeat a thump in our playful parade,
We march through the mess that our lives have made.
Lost in the shuffle, yet never askew,
Every misstep brings me closer to you.

So here's to the bumps and the rumbles we face,
On this peculiar journey without any trace.
With giggles like confetti in the air,
Our uncharted map shows love everywhere.

Echoes of Yesterday

In the attic, dust bunnies giggle and play,
Recollections of mischief from back in the day.
Grandma's old hat, perched up on a shelf,
Dust-mite friends join for a dance with themselves.

We've turned every mishap into a crown,
Worn with such pride, who could frown?
A collection of blunders, our scrapbook of cheer,
With laughter, we gather, our folly sincere.

The echoes of laughter ring through the halls,
As we trip on the memories that bounce off the walls.
Forgotten playdates and silly charades,
Our hearts still giggle while the time gently fades.

So let's raise a toast to the joy that we keep,
In the echoes of yesterday, tangled and deep.
For in every gaffe, there's a story to tell,
In laughter and love, we've managed so well.

Shadows of Forgotten Dreams

In shadows where quirky ideas reside,
Whispers of dreams we sort and divide.
A circus of thoughts that tumble and spin,
Each one a giggle, where do we begin?

The hammock still sways with the weight of our hopes,
Swinging through wishes, dashing with ropes.
A carousel of laughter, spinning so bright,
As we tease tomorrow with each playful bite.

Old comics and sketches gather their dust,
In the history of fun, we place our trust.
With crayons and laughter, we doodle our fate,
In this gallery of joy, it's never too late.

So let us embrace the shadows and gleam,
In the tangle of dreams, we forge our own team.
For every forgotten whim adds to the fun,
In this playful memoir, our hearts have won.

The Canvas of Silent Goodbyes

On a canvas stretched so tight,
We painted laughs, not a fight.
The chatter fades with the dusk,
Leaving memories, just a husk.

Fingers point at empty space,
Did that last joke leave a trace?
With a wink and a sly grin,
We swear we'll do this again.

Canvas now, just a wide sea,
Of chuckles echoing with glee.
But silence sits on the edge,
Hanging like a stubborn hedge.

With each brush of a goodbye,
We leave our laughter to fly.
In colors bold, tears that glint,
A masterpiece where fun was mint.

Flickers of Light in Darkened Spaces

In shadowy corners we stood,
Paying visits like we should.
Flashlight beams, the jests ignite,
Flickers laugh, banishing fright.

A dance of shadows on the wall,
With whispers that bounce and stall.
We toast to blunders in flight,
Tripping over words so light.

The room may darken and sway,
But our flickers won't betray.
We find the joy in the gloom,
When laughter bansish the gloom.

So let the shadows appear bold,
In their depths, fond tales unfold.
For in this dark, we know right,
The giggles will always ignite.

Echoes of Unfinished Sentences

In conversations, we begin,
But end up grinning, not a sin.
A pause, and then a long delay,
Leaves us guessing, 'what'd they say?'

With each hiccup in our talks,
Laughter strolls, like silly hawks.
Unfinished thoughts, we let them roam,
Finding humor in every tome.

It's comedic when we trip,
Or stutter through an awkward quip.
As phrases dangle in the air,
We smile, for they go everywhere.

So let the echoes laugh away,
In sentences that like to play.
For words unsaid or deeply felt,
Become the punchline, where we melt.

The Weight of Syllables Lost

Syllables fell like leaves in fall,
Each word stumbled, took a crawl.
In the weight of laughter we share,
Grammar's just a fun affair.

Adding 'um', a dash of 'uh',
Turns our chats into a hub.
A word misplaced, a giggle grows,
As silly doubts begin to pose.

The lost syllables find a home,
In punchlines, they gleefully roam.
We drop them like balloons on strings,
And watch as laughter sweetly clings.

So here's to all the slips and flops,
Each one bringing joy that never stops.
For in the chaos of words we tossed,
Resides the fun in what's embossed.

www.ingramcontent.com/pod-product-compliance
Ingram Content Group UK Ltd.
Pitfield, Milton Keynes, MK11 3LW, UK
UKHW020109171224
452675UK00013B/1425